THE BABY DANCE

A Drama in Two Acts

by Jane Anderson

D1798100

SAMUEL FRENCH, INC.
45 WEST 25TH STREET   NEW YORK 10010
7623 SUNSET BOULEVARD   HOLLYWOOD 90046
LONDON   *TORONTO*

IMPORTANT BILLING AND CREDIT
REQUIREMENTS

All producers of THE BABY DANCE *must* give credit to the Author of the Play in all programs distributed in connection with performances of the Play and in all instances in which the title of the Play appears for purposes of advertising, publicizing or otherwise exploiting the Play and/or a production. The name of the Author *must* also appear on a separate line, on which no other name appears, immediately following the title, and *must* appear in size of type not less than fifty percent the size of the title type.

ACKNOWLEDGMENTS

The author greatfully acknowledges the help and support of the following: Tess Ayers, Martin Gage, Susan Merson, Tony Schultz, Jackie Schultz, the Los Angeles Writers Bloc and Lucille Lortel.

CHARACTERS

WANDA — A woman in her late 20's, early 30's. She's dirt poor, has four kids and believes in God.

AL — her husband. He's about 6 foot two and looks like a refugee from a country-western band.

RACHEL — early to late 30's. She's from Los Angeles. She has a husband, a job, a house, a pool, smart friends and a good diet.

RICHARD — her husband. Early to late 30's. Short. A nice man outside of business.

RON — the lawyer.

TIME
The present, summer.
Highs are in the 90's
and the humidity is 90 percent.

PLACE
Act I: A trailer park in Louisiana.
Act II: A hospital room in Louisiana.

Script note: The symbol / means that the next speech begins at this point.

The Baby Dance was originally produced by The Pasadena Playhouse, State Theatre of California.

The play was then subsequently produced at The Williamstown Theatre Festival.

The Baby Dance was presented March 12 to April 28, 1991 by the Long Wharf Theatre, Arvin Brown, Artistic Director, M. Edgar Rosenblum, Executive Director, with the following cast (in order of appearance):

WANDA .... Linda Purl
AL .... Richard Lineback
RACHEL ....Stephanie Zimbalist
RICHARD .... Joel Polis
RON .... John Bennett Perry

Directed by:	Jenny Sullivan
Set Design by:	Marjorie Bradley Kellogg
Costume Design by:	David Murin
Lighting Design by:	Kirk Bookman
Production Stage Manager:	Tammy Taylor

LUCILLE LORTEL THEATRE

121 Christopher Street   924-8782

JOHN A. McQUIGGAN   LUCILLE LORTEL   DARYL ROTH

In Association with SUSAN DIETZ

present

THE BABY DANCE

by JANE ANDERSON

starring

RICHARD LINEBACK   JOHN BENNETT PERRY   JOEL POLIS

LINDA PURL   STEPHANIE ZIMBALIST

Scenery by	Costumes by	Lighting by
HUGH LANDWEHR	**DAVID MURIN**	**KIRK BOOKMAN**

Sound Design by	Production Stage Manager	Co-General Manager
BRENT EVANS	**TAMMY TAYLOR**	**PATRICIA BERRY**

Associate Producers

CHANTPLEURE, INC.   JAMES AND MAUREEN O'SULLIVAN CUSHING   GRACONN LTD.

Directed by

JENNY SULLIVAN

Presented at the Long Wharf Theatre, March 12 to April 28, 1991.
THE BABY DANCE was previously presented at The Williamstown Theatre Festival.
Originally produced by the Pasadena Playhouse, State Theatre of California,
Susan Dietz, Artistic Director, with Lenny Beer, Linda Purl and Stephanie Zimbalist.

The producers wish to express their appreciation to the Theatre Development Fund for its support of this production.

ACT I

Scene 1

LIGHTS UP on WANDA and AL in their cramped trailer park home in Louisiana. It's NIGHT and it's RAINING outside. A TV is on with bad reception. Wanda is six months pregnant. SHE's quietly talking on the phone while holding a cigarette. AL is stretched out on the sofa bed, drinking a beer.

WANDA. (*Into phone.*) OK, I want you all to go to bed now. (*Pause.*) I don't think that's a good idea, Honey. What did Grandma say? (*Pause.*) Lemme ask Daddy. (*To Al.*) Al, Kevin wants to sleep outside tonight.

AL. What for?

WANDA. Robbie's been wettin' the bed again.

AL. It's raining. He's gonna get a whole hell of a lot / wetter out there than he is lying in the god damn bed.

WANDA. (*Into phone.*) Honey, it's rainin', where you gonna go? (*A pause. To Al.*) He says he'll sleep in the car.

AL. Tell him he can if he locks the doors.

WANDA. (*Into phone.*) Kevin? Daddy says you can if you lock the doors and if you bundle up. You ask Grandma to give you a blanket. Put Patricia on so I can say good night ... Hello? Hello? (*SHE starts clicking the receiver.*)

AL. The phone go out?

WANDA. Yeah.

AL. Shit. I thought we had another day.

WANDA. Didn't you pay the bill?

7

AL. We didn't have it, babe.

WANDA. I didn't say goodnight to Patricia yet. I have to say goodnight to Patricia...

AL. Want me to drive you to a phone?

WANDA. No, I'll do it.

(WANDA gets her coat. SHE hands Al something that she's torn out of a newspaper.)

WANDA. I found this in the paper. I think you should take a look at this. (*Pause.*) Al?

AL. What?

WANDA. I gotta get my tubes tied.

(FADE OUT to a PROJECTION overhead:
"PREGNANT? HAPPILY MARRIED COUPLE, EDUCATED AND FINANCIALLY SECURE WANT TO GIVE HEALTHY WHITE BABY A LIFETIME OF LOVE, LAUGHTER AND SECURITY. WE CAN HELP WITH EXPENSES. CALL COLLECT."
FADE OUT.)

Scene 2

LIGHTS UP on WANDA in shorts, flip-flops and one of her nicer maternity blouses. SHE's arranging a cold cut plate of packaged ham, bologna and American cheese. A fan is blowing in one corner. It's very hot and muggy.
WE hear a CAR pull up. WANDA opens the door and looks out.

WANDA. (*Calling out.*) Hello!
WOMAN'S VOICE. Hello?
WANDA. Are you Rachel?
WOMAN'S VOICE. Wanda?
WANDA. Yes. I'm over here. Come on up. Watch your step.

(*RACHEL enters the trailer, bearing flowers and a Williams-Sonoma bag filled with stuff. SHE's tried to dress down for this meeting but she still projects enormous chic and prosperity. The two WOMEN look at each other and give a simultaneous "Hi!"*)

WANDA. Did you find your way OK from the airport?
RACHEL. No problem at all. Your directions were terrific.
WANDA. Good.
RACHEL. Very clear.
WANDA. Oh good. I'm glad. Was the traffic bad?
RACHEL. No, not at all.
WANDA. Al and I talked it over. We weren't sure if you should take I-20 or 80. I guess I-20 was the right choice.
RACHEL. Oh, yes. It got me right here.
WANDA. Well good. (*A beat.*) Is your husband coming?
RACHEL. He couldn't be here. He was held over at work.
WANDA. Oh, that's a shame.
RACHEL. But he told me to make sure to send you his regards.

WANDA. Well send my regards back to him.

RACHEL. It's so nice to finally meet you.

WANDA. It's nice to meet you too. You look a lot like your picture.

RACHEL. I do?

WANDA. It was a real nice picture.

RACHEL. Oh thank you. I feel like a mess right now.

WANDA. No, you look real nice.

RACHEL. Oh, well thank you. You look great, too. How are you feeling? Are you feeling all right?

WANDA. Oh, I'm fine.

RACHEL. Are you comfortable? Are you feeling comfortable?

WANDA. Well, yeah, I feel OK...

RACHEL. How's your back? Has it started to ache yet?

WANDA. Yeah, I'm feelin' it.

RACHEL. (*She's read this.*) Are you getting a lot of pressure on the cervix?

WANDA. The cervix...

RACHEL. The lower part.

WANDA. My lady parts. Oh yeah, I'm feeling some of that.

RACHEL. Is it bad?

WANDA. I'm used to it.

RACHEL. Is it like an ache? Like menstrual cramps?

WANDA. I don't remember menstrual cramps. I've been pregnant more than I've had my period.

RACHEL. Oh, well you're lucky. Cramps are worse. Much worse. And the water retention, my God, I gain about eighty pounds...

WANDA. Yeah, I get all that too.

RACHEL. Well, there you go. No matter what we do...

WANDA. That's right.

RACHEL. I've always told my husband, that if men had to put up with ovaries...

WANDA. Oh lord, you wouldn't hear the end of it.

RACHEL. Please, they'd be impossible.

WANDA. Yeah, they'd be something all right... (*A beat.*) Well, why don't you have a seat. I made us some lunch. Being so hot, I made us a cold-cut plate.

RACHEL. Oh, great. That sounds terrific.

WANDA. Al went out to get some cold things to drink. He ought to be back any minute.

RACHEL. Terrific. I can't wait to meet him.

WANDA. Yuh?

RACHEL. (*Handing her the flowers.*) Oh here, I brought these for you.

WANDA. Oh, thank you. Gosh. They're beautiful.

RACHEL. (*Hands Wanda a wrapped box from the Williams-Sonoma bag.*) And I got you this. If it's the wrong size let me know. It's all returnable.

WANDA. Gosh, isn't that pretty wrapping paper. I think I'll wait to open this for when Al gets back. (*The flowers.*) I better put these in something.

(*WANDA goes to the cupboard. RACHEL glances around the trailer. The heat is stifling. SHE tries to maintain a pleasant expression on her face.*)

RACHEL. How long have you lived here?

WANDA. Five years.

RACHEL. Uh-huh.

WANDA. But this is only temporary. As soon as Al finds better employment we're planning to move to a bigger place.

RACHEL. Well, you've done a lot with the space. You've done some very nice things with it.

WANDA. Oh. Thank you.

RACHEL. (*Sees some photographs.*) Are these your children?

WANDA. Yes, that's Brian and this here's Patricia and that's Kevin and little Robbie.

RACHEL. Oh they're great. They're just great looking children.

WANDA. Thank you. They're real good kids.

RACHEL. How old is Patricia?

WANDA. She's eight. She'll be nine in September.

RACHEL. Look at those long legs. Is she athletic?

WANDA. Well, she can run pretty good. She can run as fast as Kevin, which makes him mad. Kevin likes to be best in everything.

RACHEL. Richard and I both have short legs. We always said, if we ever had a kid, he'd have a waist and pair of feet.

WANDA. Well, my daddy had pretty long legs. And Al's got real long legs.

RACHEL. Isn't that great. (*A beat.*) How are they in school? Do they like school?

WANDA. Well, I guess they like it all right. Actually Kevin likes it the best of any of them. He's good at reading.

RACHEL. Great. That's great. Do you take him to the library?

WANDA. There's a library at school.

RACHEL. But you encourage him to read.

WANDA. Yeah, I don't tell him not to.

RACHEL. Are they here?

WANDA. My kids?

RACHEL. Do they live here with you?

WANDA. Well they're staying over at my mama's for now. She's got more room. She's got a yard for them to play in.

RACHEL. Oh sure, it's important. Especially if they're such active kids.

WANDA. You want something to drink? Al will be back with some sodas but if you're thirsty I could get you some water.

RACHEL. Terrific... is it tap water?

WANDA. Yes...

RACHEL. Oh. Do you have anything bottled?

WANDA. No. But if you want I could get you some.

RACHEL. No, that's all right.

WANDA. When Al comes back maybe I could send him out for some.

RACHEL. No, no, that's all right. (*A beat.*) But you might want to start getting some for yourself.

WANDA. I always thought it was kind of a gyp to pay for water when you could get it free.

RACHEL. Oh no, not at all. Bottled water is much better for you.

WANDA. Oh. Well, that's interesting. I'll have to tell Al.

(WANDA sets the cold cut plate down on the table and a plate of white bread. SHE sits down and waits for Rachel to serve herself first.)

RACHEL. Shouldn't we wait for Al?
WANDA. No, you can go right ahead.

(RACHEL looks at her plate.)

WANDA. Oh, do you want some mustard and mayonnaise?
RACHEL. No thank you. This is terrific. This is lovely. Thank you for doing this.

(RACHEL politely takes from the plate. WANDA bows her head in a quick prayer before she eats.)

RACHEL. Do you like the doctor we found you?
WANDA. Oh yes m'am, he's one of the nicest men I ever met.
RACHEL. I talked to him the other day. He says you're doing very well.
WANDA. Well, I sure like him a lot.
RACHEL. I brought you some more of those pre-natal vitamins.
WANDA. Oh. Thank you.
RACHEL. I didn't know if you needed more...
WANDA. Well, I stopped taking them, actually.
RACHEL. Why?
WANDA. They were stuffing me up.
RACHEL. Oh. They made you feel full?
WANDA. Well, yeah...
RACHEL. You mean, you lost your appetite?
WANDA. No, I couldn't take a crap. Excuse my French. I forgot the word for it.

RACHEL. Constipation.

WANDA. Constipation. That's right.

RACHEL. What did Doctor Costales say?

WANDA. He said I'm fine.

RACHEL. Did you ask him if you could stop taking the vitamins?

WANDA. We didn't talk about it. He said I'm fine and the baby's doing fine, so I didn't ask him about the vitamins.

RACHEL. The vitamins are part of the program.

WANDA. He said I'm doing fine.

RACHEL. Well, you might want to mention this to the doctor.

WANDA. I never took those things before and none of my kids have suffered for it.

RACHEL. I'm sure he'll say the same thing. In any case, it's fine, don't worry about it. It's fine.

(A beat. WANDA and RACHEL chew their food.)

RACHEL. Oh, I brought you a cassette of some music I thought you might enjoy. *(SHE hands Wanda a cassette.)* I made it up for you last night. I chose some music that's very, ah, peaceful and lovely and might be nice for you and the baby to listen to.

WANDA. Oh, uh-huh.

RACHEL. There's some Pachalbel and "Paul Horn in the Great Pyramid," which—well he's playing his flute in a pyramid. In Egypt.

WANDA. Oh.

RACHEL. It's very calming. You might want to play it when you have your quiet time. If you have a Walkman you can hold the headphones to your stomach. Do you have a Walkman?

WANDA. No.

RACHEL. You have a cassette player...

WANDA. Yeah, we did but it broke.

RACHEL. Oh. Well, maybe later today we can get one for you.

WANDA. Thank you. That'd be real nice of you.

RACHEL. Well, music is very important. Babies can hear music when they're in the womb.

WANDA. Yeah, I know that.

RACHEL. Well. Anyway. Is everything else all right? Did our lawyer send you the check for the air conditioner?

WANDA. Yes. Thank you.

RACHEL. Did you get one yet?

WANDA. Well, there wasn't quite enough for an air conditioner so we bought a fan.

RACHEL. Oh, well you should have told us.

WANDA. Well, we didn't want to put you out.

RACHEL. We don't mind. We want you to be comfortable.

WANDA. That's OK.

RACHEL. I thought we sent you five hundred dollars, that wasn't enough?

WANDA. Well, Al was the one who looked. He said they cost more.

RACHEL. Oh. Well how much more?

WANDA. I don't know. You can ask him when he comes back.

RACHEL. All right. (*A beat.*) Oh, I brought some pictures. (*Reaching into the Williams-Sonoma bag.*) I wanted to show you the baby's room. (*Hands some photographs to Wanda.*)

WANDA. Oh my gosh, isn't this cute? What a cute room. I like the crib. I like how it matches everything.

RACHEL. The crib is built so it turns into a bed later on.

WANDA. Hey, that's a nice changing table.

RACHEL. That will turn into a bureau.

WANDA. Isn't that neat.

RACHEL. Well, it's practical.

WANDA. I like how it all matches.

RACHEL. It's a very happy room. We chose the room with the most sun.

WANDA. You don't want the room to get too hot though. Babies are real sensitive to the heat.

RACHEL. It's a southern exposure.

WANDA. Uh-huh. You gotta put curtains up.

RACHEL. We are.

WANDA. It's important to cover the windows when the baby is taking a nap. If it's too bright they get fitful.

RACHEL. We're getting curtains. I have them on order.

WANDA. And keep the baby cool. It's dangerous for them to overheat. Don't leave the baby in the car or anything.

RACHEL. No, of course not. My God, I wouldn't do that.

WANDA. You'd be surprised. I know a lot of women who have.

RACHEL. Well, it's a very stupid thing to do.

WANDA. It's more than stupid, it's sinful.

RACHEL. I hope you don't think I would ever do anything like that.

WANDA. No, of course not, no. But you wouldn't believe what some women do. There was a woman in the trailer court here who was cooking something on the stove, right? She went out for a minute to go to the laundromat, left her baby, the trailer caught fire and the baby burned to death. Al and me were both working when it happened. I gave her some clothes. She didn't have nothing left.

RACHEL. My God.

WANDA. She was one of them welfare mothers. They're not very bright. They don't know how to take care of their kids.

RACHEL. Well, if you aren't well educated...

WANDA. They got a flaw. They have a flaw somewhere that makes them irresponsible. And it's mostly the coloreds that got the problem.

RACHEL. Well, I don't know if you can say that. Maybe this particular woman was this way.

WANDA. I know a lot of them, and they're just as bad.

RACHEL. Wanda, I don't know if you can really make a generalization like that. I think poverty is really more the issue than race...

WANDA. Do you know any of these people? You live next door to any of them?

RACHEL. No...

WANDA. No. Well you wouldn't stick up for them if you did. They sit on their behinds while their kids are running around wild, breaking up things and the men are never around except to come by and cause trouble. / We got our trailer broken into three times.

RACHEL. Well, I just think that poverty causes a lot of despair which breaks down the family unit and causes this kind of behavior.

WANDA. Uh-huh. Do you want dessert?

RACHEL. Sure.

WANDA. I made some Jello with topping. I thought it'd keep us cool.

RACHEL. Do you have any fruit?

WANDA. I got some peaches. Would you like that?

RACHEL. I love peaches. That would be perfect.

WANDA. *(Gets out a container of canned peaches.)* They're kinda warm. I could stick them in the freezer to cool them up for you.

RACHEL. You know what? You don't have to do that. I'll have the Jello.

WANDA. Are you sure? It's no trouble.

RACHEL. No, the Jello would be perfect.

WANDA. I think you'll like it better. It's more refreshing.

(WANDA sets two cups of bright red Jello on the table and spoons some Cool Whip on top of each.)

RACHEL. I brought some other pictures. I don't know if you want to see them...

WANDA. No, it's OK. I love looking at pictures.

RACHEL. *(The Jello.)* Thank you, this is lovely. *(Handing Wanda a photo.)* This is our back yard. We thought it'd be a nice play area.

WANDA. Oh, isn't that neat.

RACHEL. What I like about it, is that we're in an area with a lot of old trees. I love this tree here. Richard's going to hang a swing from it.

WANDA. What's this in the corner here?

RACHEL. Where?

WANDA. Behind the bush. Is that a pool?

RACHEL. Oh. Yes.

WANDA. Isn't that neat. I've always wanted to have a pool.

RACHEL. We're going to be very careful with the baby, make sure she doesn't get near it without being watched.

WANDA. When she grows up she'll be able to swim in it every day.

RACHEL. Swimming is wonderful exercise.

WANDA. There's a public pool around here. But it gets so crowded you got to get there early and sign up or else they don't let you in. We set up a sprinkler for the kids. It helps to cool them off at least.

RACHEL. Oh, sure sprinklers are great. I used to play in the sprinkler when I was a kid.

(THEY both taste their Jello dessert.)

RACHEL. Oh, this is very good.

WANDA. It's the red raspberry. It's one of their better flavors.

RACHEL. My mother used to make me Jello.

WANDA. Oh really?

RACHEL. Oh, sure. When I was sick. Jello is very comforting.

WANDA. I give my kids Jello all the time. It's good for them. It's supposed to make their nails strong.

RACHEL. Oh, it does. You know, sometimes I buy the plain gelatin base without the sugar. Knox makes it.

WANDA. Yeah but the kids won't take it like that. They want something that tastes good.

RACHEL. Well, if you mix it with a little fruit juice...

WANDA. Honey, it don't matter. No matter what you give 'em, kids only want to eat certain things. The only thing Kevin will eat is Sloppy Joe mix. Doesn't matter what else you put in front of him, if it isn't Sloppy Joe mix, he won't eat it.

RACHEL. Did you breast feed...?

WANDA. I breast fed some. But bottles are more convenient.

RACHEL. That's what my mother always said. But they're finding out that a lot of these formulas have sugar in them.

WANDA. Well, the formula I've used has always worked. None of my babies had any problems. They gained twice their weight in the first six months.

RACHEL. Uh-huh.

WANDA. You're gonna have to use formula.

RACHEL. My doctor recommended a special brand.

WANDA. The name brands are just as good.

RACHEL. Well, my doctor says this one is very good.

WANDA. Do you know anyone else who's used this formula?

RACHEL. No. Most of my friends breast feed.

WANDA. Uh-huh. Well my advice is to stick to the name brands. They've been around for years and you know they work. That's what I would use.

RACHEL. Well, let me think about it.

WANDA. You want some coffee or anything?

RACHEL. Do you have decaf?

WANDA. I could go next door. I think one of my neighbors has some Sanka.

RACHEL. No, that's fine.

WANDA. I'm gonna re-heat a little for myself. The baby makes me sleepy this time of day.

RACHEL. Wanda... (*SHE stops herself.*)

WANDA. Yes?

RACHEL. Uh, did you talk to Dr. Costales about drinking coffee?

WANDA. Yes.

RACHEL. What did he say?

WANDA. He said I could have it in moderation.

RACHEL. He said you could have regular coffee? Not decaf?

WANDA. Yuh.

(*WANDA starts to clear the table.*)

RACHEL. Here let me help you.

WANDA. No, you're my guest. There shouldn't be too many of us moving around in here anyway. It'll just make it hotter.

RACHEL. You sure?

WANDA. I'm fine. Why don't you sit and relax.

(*RACHEL is feeling stifled by the heat.*)

WANDA. Want me to turn up the fan?

RACHEL. Yes. Please.

WANDA. (*Turns up the fan and points it at Rachel.*) If you rub an ice cube on your wrists it'll help to cool you off. Here let me get you one.

RACHEL. Thank you. Wanda, I think while I'm here I'd like to see if we could talk to Dr. Costales together.

WANDA. Why? I've been getting along fine going down on my own.

RACHEL. I know. But I'd like us to see the doctor together.

WANDA. I don't know what for. I know about having a baby. If I know anything, I know about having babies.

RACHEL. Wanda, I know. But we all have to be aware that you aren't the only one involved here.

WANDA. I'm not going to mess up your baby.

RACHEL. That's not what I was saying. (*Taking another tack.*) Wanda, this baby is a real gift to us. You're giving us a wonderful gift. And both Richard and I can't thank you enough for that.

(WANDA stares off.)

RACHEL. Wanda?

WANDA. Yeah?

RACHEL. Are you sure you want to do this? You should tell me now. You should tell me now if you don't want to go through with this.

WANDA. No, I want to do it.

RACHEL. Are you sure? I'd rather know now then later. I really would, Wanda.

WANDA. I'm not gonna change my mind.

RACHEL. I'm not saying that you will.

WANDA. Lady, I don't have any other choice.

RACHEL. I hope you know that we're going to give this baby a lot of love.

WANDA. Look, I can give the baby love. That's not the problem. I know how to give love. You don't understand, but kids want things. They see other kids with bikes and stuff and they wonder why they can't have that too. That's what we have the problem with.

RACHEL. Is your husband feeling all right about this?

WANDA. Oh yeah, he pretty much knows there's no other way out for us.

RACHEL. Uh-huh. How about your mother?

WANDA. Well, I haven't discussed it with her yet. She'll be staying with the kids when I'm at the hospital. I'm just gonna tell her it was stillborn.

RACHEL. I'm sorry you have to go through this. I know how hard this is for you.

WANDA. No you don't. I don't mean that as an insult. But you just don't.

RACHEL. No... I just wish I could make this easier. That's all.

WANDA. I keep saying to Al that as soon as we get some extra money I wanna go in and get my tubes tied. I talked to your lawyer about possibly paying for the operation.

RACHEL. Oh, well, I don't know anything about that. (*A beat.*) Wanda, do you ever use birth control?

WANDA. Well, yeah...

RACHEL. Well do you use it all the time, or most of the time, or some of the time...

WANDA. I use it as much as I can.

RACHEL. What do you use?

WANDA. Diaphragm. But Al sometimes doesn't give me time to put it in. I try to make him wear protection but he says he "don't want to wear no overcoat."

RACHEL. Maybe you should go on the pill.

WANDA. Pill don't work, seems to me. No, I think the problem is, I'm too fertile for birth control.

RACHEL. No, I think you have to get a little tougher with old Al.

WANDA. Well, he's a man, what are you gonna do?

RACHEL. Have you thought of maybe not going through with all these pregnancies?

WANDA. Lord, I could never do that. It would haunt me to the rest of my days knowing that I killed my own baby.

RACHEL. No, I understand. I can understand that.

WANDA. There's another woman wanted my baby. She told me she had two abortions when she was younger. Now she can't have a baby. I think this was God's way of telling her she did a sinful thing.

RACHEL. Well, that's a tough one, Wanda...

WANDA. Do you and your husband go to church?

RACHEL. No.

(WANDA doesn't say anything.)

RACHEL. But Richard and I believe in spirituality. It's just that at this point in our lives, we don't take part in the organized part of religion. But of course we'd want our child to be aware of the various religious options...

WANDA. Uh-huh.

RACHEL. What denomination are you?

WANDA. We're Lutheran.

RACHEL. Oh. Uh-huh. Well, I think that's great. I was brought up Protestant. And Richard is Jewish.

WANDA. Yeah, I know that.

RACHEL. Oh. Good.

WANDA. I don't care as long as you celebrate Christmas. I think it's important for a child to have that.

RACHEL. Oh, sure, we celebrate Christmas. We always have a small tree.

WANDA. Will you have Santy Claus?

RACHEL. Yes.

WANDA. Good. I'm glad you believe in that.

RACHEL. Oh, we do.

WANDA. And what about Easter, do you do that? Come on.

RACHEL. Well, sure, we'll dye some eggs.

WANDA. Good.

RACHEL. We'll also celebrate Passover.

WANDA. Uh-huh.

RACHEL. Oh, it's a wonderful event. We have a Seder which is a special dinner where we celebrate the ah, the Jews escaping from Egypt. But it's more than a strictly Jewish event, it's celebrating the concept of freedom and liberation and...some of our non-Jewish friends attend. Someday you'll have to... if you ever have the chance you should go to a Seder. It's... anyway... I'm glad we talked about this.

WANDA. Me, too.

(A beat.)

RACHEL. You know, I've been dying to ask...can I feel the baby?

WANDA. Sure, go ahead.

RACHEL. You don't mind?

WANDA. That's what it's there for.

(WANDA scoots back in her chair. RACHEL lays her hand on her belly.)

RACHEL. Oh my God. Is that her moving?

WANDA. The baby's pretty quiet right now. It usually starts to kick up when I'm laying down.

RACHEL. I think I feel something. Oh my God, there she is I feel her. (*A beat.*) She just kicked. I felt her foot.

WANDA. No, I think it's just gas. (*Getting up.*) Would you excuse me for a minute? I got to use the ladies' room.

RACHEL. Sure.

(WANDA disappears into the small bathroom.
RACHEL collapses, overwhelmed by the heat.
WE hear a CAR with a bad engine drive up. The DOOR
slams and a DOG begins barking.
We hear, very rapidly, overlapping each other:)

AL. (*Offstage.*) Hey! You keep that sonnabitch dog on a sonnabitch leash or I'll pop the sonnabitch!

MAN'S VOICE. (*Offstage.*) Hey, you think you the landowner? / You think you *own* this place?

WOMAN'S VOICE. (*Offstage.*) Leave our / dog alone!

AL. (*Offstage.*) That God damn dog came after my kids. / I'm gonna put that dog away.

WOMAN'S VOICE. (*Offstage.*) / He did not! Fuck you!

MAN'S VOICE. (*Offstage.*) You got rights over this section? Huh? You telling me what to do?

(We hear AL viciously kicking a GARBAGE CAN.)

MAN'S VOICE. (*Offstage.*) Fucker.

AL. (*Offstage.*) Fuck you!

(The screen door swings open. It's AL, lugging a six-pack of beer, Coke and 7-Up. HE's so tall that he has to stoop a little to fit in the trailer. He's wearing his best shirt but it's already sticking to his back in the heat. He's been out drinking but as soon as he sees Rachel HE shifts to his best behavior.)
RACHEL gets up.)

RACHEL. Hello. Are you Al?

AL. Hello.

RACHEL. *(Extending her hand.)* Rachel Lieberman, nice to meet you.

AL. *(Shifts the cans to his other hand and shakes her hand.)* Nice to meet you. 'Scuse my hand. It's wet from the cans.

RACHEL. That's all right. Actually it felt good. Being that it was cold. From the cans.

AL. Oh. Yeah, it's hot in'it?

RACHEL. Yeah, it's hot. The humidity...

AL. You caught us in a heat wave. Wish't I coulda made the weather better for you but I don't have a lot of pull with the weatherman.

RACHEL. Well, neither do I. What can you do?

AL. Not much. Well let me get you something cold to whet your whistle.

(WANDA emerges from the bathroom.)

WANDA. *(To Al.)* Hi honey, where've you been to?

AL. None of the stores had anything cold. I had to drive clear to Ruston.

WANDA. Pizza Hut didn't have any?

AL. No, they were all out.

WANDA. They've never been before.

AL. Well they were. *(Turning to Rachel.)* What would you like to have, Rachel?

RACHEL. If you have a diet soda...

AL. 7-up OK?

RACHEL. Sure.

AL. *(To Wanda.)* What do you want, babe?

WANDA. Coke cola.

RACHEL. Wanda, do you want my 7-up?

WANDA. No thank you. I'd rather have a Coke.

AL. *(To Rachel.)* So you get down here O.K.?

RACHEL. Just fine. Didn't take long at all.

AL. Directions OK?

RACHEL. They were terrific.

WANDA. I was telling Rachel that we were trying to decide which would be a better route for her to take. Turns out we picked the right one.

AL. Oh yeah? *(Handing Wanda and Rachel their sodas.)* Here you go, Ladies.

RACHEL. Thank you, Al.

(AL pops himself a beer.)

AL. *(To Rachel.)* If you don't mind, I'm gonna have myself a beer. Best thing there is for a thirst. Sure you don't want one?

RACHEL. Well it sure sounds good, but I'm gonna pass. If I have a beer in the middle of the afternoon I fall asleep.

AL. That doesn't matter, you can take a nap here if you like.

WANDA. Al, she doesn't want a beer.

AL. (*To Wanda.*) I was just makin' an offer, babe. (*Back to Rachel.*) How long you here for?

RACHEL. I have to be back at work on Monday so I'm flying back tomorrow night.

AL. Uh-huh. So I hear you're in the movie business.

RACHEL. I'm in development.

AL. You develop things?

RACHEL. That's right. I put together projects.

AL. Uh-huh. Your husband do that too?

RACHEL. He's in the financial end of it. He's vice president of business affairs.

AL. Uh-huh.

WANDA. (*To Rachel.*) Have you ever met Don Johnson?

RACHEL. No.

AL. Wanda chose you 'cause she thought you could introduce her to movie stars.

WANDA. (*Slapping at him.*) That's not true.

AL. (*Teasing.*) Yeah, she did. Thought she'd come out and visit you, see Don Johnson sittin' in your living room.

WANDA. A-AL...

RACHEL. Well, I only know writers.

WANDA. Oh, that's OK.

AL. So, I've always wondered. How much does it take to make a movie, coupla million?

RACHEL. Well anywhere from four million to thirty million for the bigger movies.

AL. Holy shii... cow. You get a cut off the movies you make?

RACHEL. No.

AL. Who does?

RACHEL. The producers. And the studio. But my husband and I don't have anything to do with that.

AL. Uh-huh.

WANDA. We haven't been to the movies in so long. Daddy, what's that last movie we saw, we took the kids?

AL. I dunno.

WANDA. I think it was *Caddyshack*. Who was in that? He has those buggy eyes, he's real funny...I forget. Anyway, / it was a real cute movie...

AL. I've been to Los Angeles once. Friend of mine out there was in the music business. He was interested in making a record with me.

RACHEL. Oh, really?

WANDA. He wanted Al to put up half the money.

AL. (*To Wanda.*) That's called investing, babe.

WANDA. Yeah, but we didn't have nothin' to invest.

RACHEL. Do you sing, Al?

AL. Yeah, I've pitched my pipes here and there.

WANDA. Al sings real good. He sang in a band once.

RACHEL. That's wonderful. What band?

WANDA. The Dean Tully band?

RACHEL. Uh-huh.

WANDA. They're local. Well, they're in Shreveport.

RACHEL. That's terrific. (*To Al.*) What kind of music do you sing?

AL. Country, Rock. Country-Rock. A little bit of everything.

RACHEL. Do you come from a musical family?

AL. I don't know if you'd call them musical...

WANDA. Grandma Brenna is musical.

AL. Yeah, but she's pretty bad. (*To Rachel.*) She has one of them electric organs.

WANDA. She can sight-read anything you put in front of her.

RACHEL. That's a real gift. I took piano lessons when I was a kid but it takes me three hours to figure out the fingering on five lousy notes. Richard is the same way.

WANDA. Patricia has a musical talent.

RACHEL. Oh, really?

WANDA. She sings in the glee club.

RACHEL. That's great.

WANDA. I wish we could give her piano lessons. I think she'd have a real feel for it.

RACHEL. Really.

AL. Well hey, why don't we give Patricia to Rachel, too. We could make it a two-for-one deal.

WANDA. Al, that's not funny. (*SHE takes Al's beer from him.*)

WANDA. (*To Rachel.*) You want me to freshen up your 7-up?

RACHEL. Thank you.

WANDA. I'll see if we have any ice left.

RACHEL. (*To Al.*) Wanda says you didn't have enough for an air conditioner. Were you able to price a couple?

AL. Oh yeah. There was several models I looked at.

RACHEL. How much do they cost?

AL. See, the problem is the voltage. We don't have enough voltage here to accommodate a regular unit. So we got to get a generator.

RACHEL. I see. Have you priced any?

AL. Well, they run about four, five hundred dollars a piece for the good ones and the air conditioner runs about the same.

(RACHEL doesn't say anything.
WANDA hands her the 7-up.)

RACHEL. Thank you.

AL. It's been hot. It's been a real hot summer. Only way we've been able to cool off is to sit in the Pizza Hut.

RACHEL. So how much more do you think you'll need?

(AL looks to Wanda.)

WANDA. I have to visit the bathroom again. I'll be right back. *(WANDA leaves.)*

AL. Well, let's see. We kept what you gave us minus the thirty dollars for the fan. And I had to make an emergency repair on my car. That took us back about eighty dollars.

RACHEL. The money was supposed to be for an air conditioner.

AL. I know. But the brake pads were worn and it was getting real dangerous. I figured you wouldn't want me to be driving Wanda under conditions like that.

RACHEL. I really should be doing this through our lawyer.

AL. Oh. Of course.

(A beat.)

RACHEL. I'll write you a check for six hundred dollars, will that cover it?

AL. Yeah, I think it will.

RACHEL. *(Gets out her check book.)* So where do you come from, Al? Did you grow up around here?

AL. I grew up in Gibsland.

RACHEL. Uh-huh. Is that near here?

AL. 'Bout twenty miles.

RACHEL. Do your parents still live there?

AL. My mama does. My daddy isn't alive anymore.

RACHEL. When did he pass away?

AL. 'Bout fifteen years ago.

RACHEL. Oh. Was it something... did he have something internal?

AL. Car crash.

RACHEL. Oh. I'm sorry.

AL. Got cut in half by the windshield. They took pictures of him and then used them in those driver ed movies.

RACHEL. Jesus.

AL. They didn't ask us permission or anything. Seems they should give us money for it. You know anything about that?

RACHEL. I don't know about residuals for educational films. But I could talk to my lawyer.

AL. Yeah, I think they're still showing it.

(WANDA comes out of the bathroom.)

WANDA. False alarm. *(To Rachel.)* When the baby's sittin' on your bladder, you don't know if you're coming or going.

RACHEL. Al was telling me about his father.

WANDA. Oh. Yeah.

RACHEL. (*To Al.*) Do you have brothers or sisters?

AL. Four sisters, three brothers.

RACHEL. My God, there were eight of you?

AL. Yeah.

RACHEL. How did all of you manage?

AL. We worked.

WANDA. That's why Al couldn't finish high school.

AL. Thank you for telling her that.

WANDA. She knew already, Al.

RACHEL. Ron, our lawyer told us...

AL. Uh-huh.

RACHEL. But I can understand the circumstances. It's very easy to call someone a dropout, but there are reasons behind it. I really don't believe it has anything to do with intelligence or drive.

WANDA. That's right. Al didn't have a chance.

AL. Hey, I'm doin' all right.

WANDA. That's 'cause you're strong. What about Earl who's living with his wife and kid in a car? What about Frank?

AL. Well, Frank's just Frank.

WANDA. (*To Rachel.*) Frank has a drinking problem and he goes out and shoots people's dogs.

AL. Only the ones that bark all night.

WANDA. I know why he does it. He didn't grow up right. Al told me they all had to fight for places to sleep at night. Frank was so timid he couldn't even get a place on the couch. All the other kids would / push him off.

AL. It wasn't that bad.

WANDA. And their mother couldn't handle them, she was too spent just from makin' ends meet.

AL. She got through it.

WANDA. She's got a sadness, Al.

AL. So? Who don't? Hell, I bet even folks in Los Angeles got a sadness. Rachel how 'bout it? You got any sadness?

WANDA. Al, come on.

AL. Well I bet she does. Every woman has a little sadness. That's what makes them so pretty. *(To Rachel.)* Am I right?

RACHEL. Well gee, I never thought about that, Al.

AL. Well whatever it is you have, you have it in the right combination.

RACHEL. Well, thank you. Anyway... *(Handing the check to Wanda.)* This is for the air conditioner...

AL. *(Taking the check before it reaches Wanda.)* Actually, our bank account is under my name and it'll be a lot easier to cash it if it's made out to me.

RACHEL. We've been making out all our checks to Wanda.

AL. Yeah, but it's been a real hassle, depositing and switching the money over, and all that.

RACHEL. Uh-huh.

AL. It'd just be easier.

RACHEL. I'm sorry, I can only make the checks out to Wanda.

WANDA. It's the rule, honey. Everybody has to do it that way.

AL. *(To Rachel.)* I'm her husband.

RACHEL. Al, I understand. It's hard. This is new territory for all of us and there can be a lot of misunderstandings. But this is why we had Ron set up a system for dealing with things like this.

(AL doesn't say anything.)

RACHEL. Are you OK about this Al?

AL. Yuh.

RACHEL. Anyway... *(To Wanda.)* I should head back to the hotel and make some calls.

WANDA. Oh, I have to open your present.

RACHEL. Oh, right. *(As WANDA gets the present.)* I hope it's the right size. If it isn't I'll return it and send you another.

(WANDA starts peeling the wrapping off, trying not to tear the paper. SHE's taking forever.)

RACHEL. *(Barely audible.)* Oh, come on.

WANDA. *(Opens the box and pulls out a designer maternity shift.)* Oh, it's just beautiful.

RACHEL. Do you like it?

WANDA. I've never seen maternal wear this nice. I'd wear this even if I weren't pregnant.

RACHEL. Actually, it has a special panel, you can turn it into a regular dress after you're done.

WANDA. Oh isn't that neat. Hey Daddy, did you hear that? It turns into a regular dress later on.

AL. Uh-huh.

WANDA. *(To Rachel.)* Can I try it on?

RACHEL. Absolutely. Go ahead.

(WANDA takes the dress into the bathroom. Rachel is left with Al.)

RACHEL. So when do you think you can put in the air conditioning?

AL. Some time next week.

RACHEL. I think the sooner the better...

AL. Yeah, I said I'd get it in.

RACHEL. Good.

AL. So which one of you is the one can't have a baby?

RACHEL. Excuse me?

AL. Is it you or your husband can't have a baby?

RACHEL. Gee, Al, that's kind of personal information.

AL. You know everything you want to know about us. We have a right to know certain things about you.

RACHEL. Well, I can understand your point. But there are certain things that Richard and I consider confidential.

AL. Is he the one? He the one can't reproduce?

RACHEL. No.

AL. Uh-huh. So what's wrong with you?

RACHEL. I'm not going to get into that.

AL. I don't mean to get personal or anything.

RACHEL. Well, you are.

AL. I've just never been around a woman who couldn't get pregnant before. Seems all the women I know, you don't have to look at 'em twice, but next thing you know they're walkin' around big as a cow.

(RACHEL doesn't say anything.)

AL. I meant that as a compliment. What I meant to say is that you look better than most women around here. You look like you pay better attention to yourself. I'm just saying that I think your husband's lucky.

RACHEL. Well Al, that's another way of looking at it.

AL. Want another 7-up or anything?

(RACHEL shakes her head.
We hear heavy RAP MUSIC blaring outside. AL walks to the door and yells out.)

AL. Hey! Turn it down!

(The MUSIC gets louder.)

AL. HEY! (*Slams the door shut.*) Damn welfare niggers. They play their nigger music all day long. Don't have no consideration for the rest of us.

(RACHEL is disgusted with Al. HE catches her look.)

AL. Hey, that's what they call each other. I hear them using it all the time.

RACHEL. I'm sorry, but if you're white, you don't have any right to use that word.

AL. I guess you're into civil rights.

RACHEL. Yes I am.

AL. (*Trying to joke them out of it.*) Hey, we're just a bunch of dumb rednecks down here. We don't know any better.

RACHEL. Well, now you do.

AL. Excuse me, can I ask you a question? If you're into civil rights, then how come you advertised for a white baby? How come you're paying so much for a white baby when you could of gotten a black baby for free?

RACHEL. (*After a beat.*) You're right, Al. You're absolutely right. (*SHE wipes the sweat off her face.*) Could you open the door please? It's very hot in here.

(*AL opens the door. The MUSIC blasts in.*)

AL. See what I'm talking about?

(*WANDA re-emerges from the bathroom wearing the new dress. THEY have to shout above the music.*)

RACHEL. Oh, let me see. How does it fit?
WANDA. It fits really good.
RACHEL. It looks cute on you. Do you like it?
WANDA. Yeah, I like it a lot. What kind of material is it?
RACHEL. Cotton. It's all cotton.
WANDA. It feels good. It's nice and cool.

(*The MUSIC is pounding.*)

WANDA. Al, could you ask them to turn that down? It's giving me a headache.
AL. (*Gets up and shouts out the door.*) Hey! Shut that music up! Hey!

(*It gets louder. Suddenly RACHEL jumps up and screams out the door.*)

RACHEL. HEY! THERE'S A PREGNANT WOMAN
IN HERE! TURN THAT FUCKING MUSIC DOWN!!!

(The MUSIC turns off.)

    WANDA. Well, I guess you told them.
    RACHEL. Yeah, I guess I did.
    WANDA. I didn't know you used words like that.
    RACHEL. Oh I do.
    AL. Wanda, she kept saying, "Al, you better clean up
your mouth before Rachel comes. She's not gonna like it
if you / use dirty words."
    WANDA. I didn't say that.
    AL. Yes she did. She was all over my back about it.
    RACHEL. Well my language can get pretty bad.
    AL. Hey, I believe it. Boy, you didn't hold back, just
shut them Afro-Americans right up.

(A beat.)

    RACHEL. Wanda, I'm going to try to get a hold of
Doctor Costales and see if he can meet with us tomorrow.
What's a good time for you?
    WANDA. Any time is OK.
    RACHEL. What time do you get out of church?
    WANDA. Oh. Um, about noon, I guess. Or eleven. I
could get out earlier if you want.
    RACHEL. If I get an earlier appointment do you want
me to pick you up at your church?
    WANDA. No, you could pick me up here...

AL. (*To Wanda.*) I don't know who you're tryin' to impress. When's the last time you been to church? 'Scuse me. I gotta take a leak. (*HE exits to the bathroom.*)

WANDA. I haven't been going to church lately. It just makes me uncomfortable to sit for too long.

RACHEL. I understand.

WANDA. And, well, I'm just uncomfortable being there right now.

RACHEL. Well, anyway, I don't think Dr. Costales could see us any earlier than eleven. I'll call him and see what he says.

WANDA. OK.

RACHEL. I'll call you as soon as I know.

WANDA. Can I call you?

RACHEL. Is your phone not working again?

WANDA. Well, you know, off and on.

RACHEL. I thought we gave you money for the phone bill.

(WANDA doesn't say anything.)

RACHEL. What happened to the money, Wanda?

WANDA. Well, my mom got into trouble for writing some bad checks. We had to use the money for bail. We figured it was all right to use the the phone money since we need my mom to help take care of the other kids.

(A long beat. AL comes out of the bathroom. HE notices the tension.)

AL. What, I wasn't supposed to say the word "leak"?

WANDA. (*To AL.*) We were talking about the phone bill.

AL. Oh, yeah. (*To Rachel.*) We had to shift some of the money around. We had some unforeseen difficulties.

WANDA. I told her, Al.

AL. Oh.

RACHEL. You know, I get this feeling that both of you have this image of Richard and me, this image that we're very wealthy people with an unlimited supply of money. Now whether we can actually afford to give you all this money is not the point. Although I'd like you to know that in this one month we have already spent more than the money we saved for this child's first year of college. But the real point, the real point is that I'm starting to feel used. This baby means everything to me, I love this baby and I don't want to think that she's being used as a bargaining tool...

WANDA. (*Jumping on Rachel.*) Shut your mouth! You shut your mouth! You're the one put the ad in the paper! You're the one's been talking money!

AL. (*To Rachel.*) Hey, lady, if you want to call this thing / off. I don't give a shit...

WANDA. (*To Rachel.*) And don't tell me you love this baby! How can you say you love her when you haven't even felt her kick? You won't know her 'till I give her to you. She's my baby right now and don't you / forget it!

RACHEL. Then treat that baby right for God's sake! Why the hell are you putting all that crap in your body?!

AL. Lay off her / about that.

WANDA. Listen, whatever I want to put in my / body is *my* business.

RACHEL. (*Yelling at Al.*) She's drinking *coffee* for Christ sake!

AL. So what?

WANDA. The doctor said I could!

RACHEL. Bullshit, Wanda, he did not! What's wrong with you? Are you living in a / box?

AL. (*To Rachel.*) Back off her.

RACHEL. I know you watch TV. Do you ever listen to the news? Do you ever listen to the reports? Or do you just not care because you're giving this baby to someone else.

WANDA. *Fuck you lady! Fuck you!* You think I'd hurt my own babies?! You think I'm such trash, I don't care what happens to my / babies?!

AL. (*Trying to pull Wanda back.*) Cool out, baby, she ain't worth it.

WANDA. Shut up, Al! (*To Rachel.*) And don't go giving me sob stories about money. You got money, you got plenty of money 'cause whatever you don't have, you can just go out and buy it!

RACHEL. You have no idea, *no* idea what a horrible thing that is to say to me.

(*RACHEL grabs her things and walks out. WANDA starts sobbing hysterically and pounding Al's chest. AL helps her into her chair.*)

AL. That's OK, baby, that's OK. Everyone got all worked up. Just try to cool out. (*Giving Wanda kisses.*) That feel good? That feel good, honey?

RACHEL. (*Quietly re-enters and stands near the door.*) I just came back to say that I'm sorry this happened. I don't know what I expected, but obviously this is not going to work out. I'd like to pay for the rest of your health care. And the hospital expenses. That's how I'd like to settle it.

AL. Yeah, I think that's pretty fair.

WANDA. No. I want her to have the baby.

AL. She doesn't want it, Wanda.

WANDA. I want her to have it. Rachel c'mere. C'mere and feel the baby. She's movin' around.

RACHEL. No.

WANDA. Al, bring Rachel over here to me.

AL. She don't want to.

WANDA. Rachel, please don't be mad at me. I didn't mean what I said to you. I want you to have my baby.

AL. Wanda, cool out, OK?

WANDA. Al, go outside. I want to be alone with Rachel for a minute.

AL. There's nothing to talk to her about. We're keeping the baby.

WANDA. Come on, Al, just leave us alone for a minute.

RACHEL. I can't take this child, Wanda.

WANDA. Why not?

AL. 'Cause she changed her mind.

WANDA. Al, shut up.

AL. Hey, don't say shut up to me.

RACHEL. I can't take the baby. You're too conflicted about this, Wanda.

WANDA. No I'm not. I made up my mind.

AL. Wanda, it's over. She don't want it.

WANDA. Yes she does! Just shut up for a minute, will you?

(AL hits Wanda.)

AL. Hey! Don't say shut up to me, you understand?

RACHEL. How dare you hit a pregnant woman! How dare you!

AL. She's all right. I didn't hurt her. (*To Wanda.*) You OK, Baby?

WANDA. Al, go away. Just go outside. Daddy, please. Just go outside.

(AL grabs his keys and exits.
WE hear him kick at the CANS.)

RACHEL. Are you all right?

WANDA. Oh yeah, I'm fine. He never hits hard. It's all for show.

RACHEL. You want me to take you back to the hotel?

WANDA. No, I got to cook supper for the kids tonight. (*The WOMEN stop to listen to the sound of Al's CAR squealing around the courtyard and driving away.*) It's so hot, maybe I'll make everyone sandwiches. And then my mama and me have to go to the laundromat.

RACHEL. Wanda, does he hit your children?

WANDA. Al? No, not out of meanness. When he gets mad. You know, when the kids get on his nerves.

RACHEL. Uh-huh.

WANDA. It's not genetic or nothing. It's just how he was raised. You know, it don't matter where a baby comes from. You can make them turn out however you want. A brand new baby's too excited to be alive to care about what was going on when it was sitting in its mama's belly. (*WANDA takes Rachel's hand and puts it on her stomach.*)

Feel that? She's stretching her legs. They're gettin' to be so long, she's running out of room in there.

(RACHEL tries to take her hand away. WANDA holds it there.)

WANDA. You feel her kicking? She's thinking about swimming in her own pool in her own back yard and how her new mama and daddy are gonna buy her dresses and pretty things. I think she knows where she's going 'cause I dream about it at night. I've been seeing this happy little girl at a birthday party dancing around a great big cake with all this attention being paid to her. And they start singing her the birthday song. But I never hear what her name is when they sing it at the end. Did you think of a name for her yet?

RACHEL. Yes, we did.

WANDA. If you want, you can talk to her and tell her her name. I'll shut my ears so I don't hear.

(WANDA holds her fingers over her ears and closes her eyes as RACHEL leans her head toward Wanda's belly.)

FADE OUT

ACT II

Scene 1

One month later.

LIGHTS UP on Wanda's hospital room in the maternity ward. RACHEL and her husband RICHARD burst in, schlepping briefcases, jackets, a baby carrier. THEY both look like they just ran out of business meetings. RACHEL is completely frantic. RICHARD is trying to relieve her of everything she's carrying. His dress shirt is plastered with sweat.

RICHARD. Here, give me your coat, give me your coat.

RACHEL. Where am I going?

RICHARD. Down the hall. They'll show / you.

RACHEL. What about my purse? / Should I take my purse?

RICHARD. I'll take care of it.

RACHEL. Did we order the flowers for Wanda?

RICHARD. Done.

RACHEL. Where will you be?

RICHARD. I'll be right here. Don't worry.

RACHEL. I love you.

RICHARD. I love you too. Go, go.

(RACHEL exits. RICHARD organizes their things. Then HE searches for the phone and starts to dial.)

49

RICHARD. Hello? Oh. Yes, I'm trying to dial out... I was dialing long distance... yes, I know, I'm using my credit card.

(RON, the lawyer enters. THEY signal hello.)

RICHARD. Can you tell me how to dial out?... I'm aware of that, I'm using my credit card... Yes... Thank you.

(RICHARD presses the receiver and starts punching a long complicated number. RON has taken a clean shirt out of his briefcase and is changing.)

RON. Just get here?
RICHARD. You wouldn't believe what we've been through already. Jesus, we're lucky we made it. Can you believe this heat?
RON. Ninety-five.
RICHARD. I'm not used to this humidity. *(Into phone.)* Nancy, hi, no, not yet. We just got here. Thank you. I will. Any messages? *(Taking out a pen.)* Uh-huh... .did the Midler people call? Well, let me give you my number—don't let them call here—but let me give you the number where I'm at, let me know if they called. Area code 318-555-4647, extension 8623. All right...Thanks, Nancy. *(Hangs up.)*
RON. Where's Rachel?
RICHARD. She's getting ready to go in with Wanda.
RON. How is she doing? Is she jazzed?

RICHARD. On the way over, she said she was getting sympathetic pains. She swore to God she was getting actual contractions.

RON. I've had a lot of my clients say that.

RICHARD. This is common?

RON. Oh yeah.

RICHARD. (*A little disappointed.*) Oh.

RON. How are you doing?

RICHARD. Great.

RON. Great. How was your flight?

RICHARD. Don't ask. We sat on the runway for half an hour. (*Dismissing with his hand.*) Don't ask. You were in New York?

RON. New Haven. We had a birth for some other clients—two gay women, a designer and a therapist, live in Manhattan, very nice women. Their birth mother is a college girl, single, goes to Yale. Very smart. Pre-med.

RICHARD. Uh-huh.

RON. Very sharp, believes in abortion but decided she wanted to add to the gene pool. Had a baby boy... (*Looks at watch.*) five hours ago. Just made the plane.

RICHARD. Ah.

RON. We have another girl who's in labor in Texas. They're all having them at once. I don't know what it is, someone said it's the full moon.

RICHARD. My dentist said that people bleed more during the full moon.

RON. I believe it, I believe it. The moon is a force, definitely a force.

RICHARD. This pre-med girl, did we know about her? Was she available when we were looking?

RON. Yes, I believe she was.

RICHARD. Why didn't you tell us about her?

RON. She was too short.

RICHARD. Oh.

RON. Remember, you and Rachel told me...

RICHARD. Right.

RON. Otherwise I would have brought her up.

RICHARD. No, I understand.

RON. I'm very careful if my clients give me specifics. I don't want to / waste anyone's time...

RICHARD. No, I understand. (*A beat.*) How tall was the girl?

RON. Four foot eleven.

RICHARD. Oh, yeah, well that's / way too...

RON. That's why I didn't even mention her to you.

RICHARD. No, you did the right thing. Absolutely.

RON. You're going to have a beautiful child.

RICHARD. No, we're very happy. Rachel is very excited about this. She likes Wanda. She likes her very much.

RON. Oh yeah, Wanda is a very bright girl. She's very sharp.

RICHARD. That's what Rachel says.

RON. No, I think you have a very good match. Excuse me. (*RON picks up the phone and starts dialing a long, complicated number.*)

RICHARD. You have to dial 990 to get out.

RON. Oh, thanks.

RICHARD. Did her husband call you about the car thing?

RON. No.

RICHARD. He called me last night...

(RON holds his finger up.)

RON. *(Into phone.)* Hi Linda, I'm here with the Leibermans. Did you check into the Dallas flight? *(Hands Richard some contracts from his briefcase and signals to him to read them. Into phone.)* Uh-huh...uh-huh...great. Let me give you the number here. 318-555-4647 extension... *(HE looks to Richard.)*

RICHARD. 6823.

RON. 6823...

RICHARD. *(Over this.)* 8623

RON. What?

RICHARD. 8623.

RON. *(Into phone.)* 8623. All right. I will. *(Hangs up.)* Linda said to send you and Rachel her good wishes.

RICHARD. Oh. Thank you.

RON. So you said he called you?

RICHARD. Last night. He wanted to talk about a car.

RON. I think at this point the only thing we can do is play him out.

RICHARD. He has to give consent?

RON. Legally, yes.

RICHARD. We can't have a separate contract with Wanda?

RON. No.

RICHARD. So we're talking a by-the-balls kind of thing.

(RON nods.)

RICHARD. This is sick. This is very sick.

RON. Look, nine cases out of ten, if you tell them no, they'll back off. If they press further I advise that you terminate the agreement.

RICHARD. At this point? You're kidding, at this point? And you know he knows that. This is fucking blackmail.

RON. Look, it might be worth your while to make him some kind of offer in good faith, throw down three, four thousand for a second-hand.

RICHARD. He wants a new Corvette.

RON. (*Laughing.*) Hey, so do I.

RICHARD. Jesus, last night I was even thinking of giving him my mother's old Continental, that, bless her heart she isn't driving anymore since she shrunk below the steering wheel. I was figuring, why not? I'll go out to Long Island, pick it up, drive the fifteen hundred miles back here. What the hell. I'll say, here, here you bastard, bigot-redneck, here, take my mother's Continental, all leather upholstery, whitewalls, a lighted make-up mirror for your lovely wife. Here, take the car my mother drove to temple in, my good mother who keeps saying, "Richard, why can't you get a Jewish baby" and I tell her, "but Ma, Jews are too smart. They don't have unwanted children."

RON. Let's just play it out.

RICHARD. I don't want Rachel to have to go through anymore of this crap. It's not fair. It's killing her.

RON. No, I understand.

RICHARD. You wanna yank someone's balls in business that's one thing, but to bargain with a child, it's immoral. It's animal. I'm sorry, but this is human shit we're dealing with.

RON. As I said, my hunch is, it's a bluff. He can be handled.

RICHARD. I know he can be handled. The point is. I shouldn't even have to be feeling this. Even if it is a bluff, I resent that the birth of our child is being flavored like this.

RON. Look, I've said this to you before, but the fact is, this is going to be a down-the-line kind of thing. You're still gonna get the rush, you're gonna get the rush when you hold the baby, but the "wow-we're-home-free," that will come later.

RICHARD. Was that other girl Jewish?

RON. Which one?

RICHARD. The one that went to the gay women. Was she a Jew as well?

RON. Oh. Yes, she was.

RICHARD. (*The contracts.*) So what do we have here?

RON. This is your custody agreement, this is the interstate compact agreement, the California State compact agreement. Wanda and her husband can't sign their contracts for another five days.

RICHARD. Of course, why should it be easy?

RON. The Louisiana laws are a bitch. That's why I wanted to move Wanda to another state.

RICHARD. I know, I know. Rachel didn't like the idea...

RON. No, I understand...

RICHARD. I would of made a stronger argument for it if I knew...

RON. You can make arguments both ways. I'm not saying that we did the wrong thing.

RICHARD. I'm not either.

RON. I'm just saying that the laws here are a pain in the ass.

RICHARD. I agree, my friend, I agree.

(RACHEL enters. SHE's wearing a green hospital gown. SHE's excited and flushed.)

RACHEL. Richard!

RON. Rachel, how're you doing?

RACHEL. Hello, Ron. Richard, the baby's starting to crown already. I can see the top of her head. I was the first one to see her. Please watch with me. I asked Wanda. She said it's all right. They're getting you some hospital gowns.

RICHARD. I don't know, it's... I don't know.

RACHEL. You said you would.

RICHARD. I know, but that was an abstract discussion.

RACHEL. I'd really like you to, Richard.

RICHARD. Rachel, I would if this was you but this is a woman I don't know. It's a very personal and graphic kind of thing...

RACHEL. It's birth, what do you want?

RICHARD. Rachel, if the baby was coming out of you of course I'd want to be there. But I don't know if I should be staring at some strange woman's wide-open vagina...

RACHEL. Richard, it's not a vagina anymore, it's a channel for God's sake.

RICHARD. *(To Ron.)* What do you think?

RON. It's a personal choice.

RICHARD. *(To Rachel.)* All right, if you want me to watch...

RACHEL. If you're going to be uncomfortable...

RICHARD. No, I'll do it...

RACHEL. It's not a task, it's a joy. If you're gonna make it a task, I'd rather you not do it.

RICHARD. Do you want me to be there?

RACHEL. Only if you want to.

RICHARD. I'll do it for you.

RACHEL. That's not why I want you to do it.

RICHARD. I said I'll do it.

RACHEL. I don't want you to do it for me, I want you to do it for you.

RICHARD. I would do it for you.

RACHEL. Honey, it's fine.

RICHARD. I'm being honest.

RACHEL. I know. It's fine.

RICHARD. I wish I could say that I'd be more comfortable.

RACHEL. Richard, it's fine. I love you, it's fine.

RICHARD. You sure?

RACHEL. Yeah.

RICHARD. You'll be all right if I'm out here?

RACHEL. Yes.

RICHARD. I love you.

(RACHEL slams out.)

RICHARD. *(To Ron.)* Would you want to watch?

RON. *(Immediately.)* No.

RICHARD. I'm glad I'm not the only one.

RON. No, no, not at all. I've had very few men who wanted to watch.

RICHARD. As I said, it's an intrusion.

RON. I've had a couple of actors. They wanted to watch. But for some reason the women always want to watch. Maybe because it's more familiar to them.

RICHARD. Well, it's a sympathetic kind of thing. They want to live through the act.

RON. Exactly. But for me it's too hard. Even if it were my own wife.

RICHARD. I was just thinking that.

RON. No, it's hard. Birth is a violent thing. There's a lot of blood, a lot of pain, the woman is being stretched in all directions, the baby doesn't know what's happening to it.

RICHARD. That's it. That's it exactly. I don't want to see those I love being hurt.

RON. Exactly.

(AL enters carrying some flowers.
RICHARD and RON look up.
AL nods back to them.)

RON. Al? Ron Davis. We talked on the phone.

AL. (*Looks past Ron to Richard.*) Are you Richard Leiberman?

RICHARD. Al, nice to meet you. (*HE shakes his hand.*)

(RON and AL start to say something at once.)

RON. Go ahead.
AL. So you got out here all right? The flight was OK?
RICHARD. Oh yeah, it was fine.
AL. That's good.

RICHARD. (*To Ron.*) Oh, did I tell you? When we went to get our rental car, the bastards had overbooked us. I couldn't believe it.

RON. Did you book it through the airlines?

RICHARD. Yeah.

RON. I had the same problem in Fort Worth. The airlines always screw up the rental cars.

RICHARD. Oh really?

RON. Did you talk to the airline?

RICHARD. We didn't have time, we were trying to get here.

RON. They're supposed to give you mileage points if they overbook.

RICHARD. If they overbook on the car?

RON. Oh yeah. Make sure to call them.

RICHARD. Good. I will.

(A beat.)

RON. So what can we do for you, Al?

AL. I'm just here to see Wanda. Make sure she's OK.

(RON and RICHARD nod.)

AL. What's going on? What part is she at?

RON. She's still in labor.

AL. Can I go in and see her?

RON. No.

RICHARD. We should get some coffee. Is there someone around here who can get us coffee?

RON. I think I saw a coffee machine down the hall.

RICHARD. Terrific. Al, what do you take in your coffee?

AL. Huh? Oh. Milk.

RICHARD. Ron?

RON. Black will be fine.

(AL digs in his pocket for some change.)

RICHARD. Don't worry about it. I got it. *(Exits.)*

RON. So how do you think your team's gonna do this year, Al?

AL. What?

RON. Your team. The Saints.

AL. Oh. Yeah.

RON. I've been following Bobby Herbert. *(Adjust name accordingly.)* Good arm. Great player. He's going to be great this year.

(A beat.)

AL. Excuse me, are those the contracts?

RON. Yes.

AL. Can I look at them?

RON. Of course.

(RON hands Al the contracts. AL looks at them. The language, of course, is totally incomprehensible.)

RON. We're going to have someone go over all of this with you in a few days. Did the social worker talk to you yet?

AL. Yeah, Wanda...

RON. Great. You'll also be talking to Larry Forshan, he's our attorney out here. A great guy, I think you'll like him. You like to fish?

AL. Sure.

RON. Larry's a great fisherman. Has a boat, likes to go out in the gulf.

AL. Uh-huh.

RON. He'll be contacting you but I'm going to give you his number right now, if you have any questions.

AL. Okay.

RON. (*Writing the number on a card.*) He said there's a pretty good deer population around here. You do any hunting?

AL. Yeah, I used to hunt with my uncle before he got his leg shot off.

RON. Oh. Another hunter?

AL. Yeah.

RON. Always the case. Sorry to hear that. (*Back to the contracts.*) You know, you and Wanda are in a terrific position, Al. The state gives you five days before you have to sign anything—and I'll tell you quite personally, I like this law. I like it a lot. Most states, you have twenty-four hours, that's it, papers are being shoved in your face, Wanda might be having second thoughts, you're starting to feel pressured. This way, even though you might already know this is what you want to do, you feel in control of the situation.

AL. Uh-huh.

(*RICHARD enters with three coffees.*)

RICHARD. I don't know how good this coffee is. Looks like it's been in the machine for a week.

RON. (*To Richard.*) I was telling Al that I think the five day waiting period is a very healthy part of the contract.

RICHARD. Oh, right. Absolutely. I'm all for it. (*Handing cup to Al.*) There you go Al. That enough cream?

AL. Yeah, thanks.

RICHARD. I forgot, did you want sugar?

AL. No.

RON. But as long as it's understood, Al, that after that five day period if you still don't sign the papers Richard and Rachel are under no obligation to care for either Wanda or the child.

AL. Yeah, I'm fully aware of that.

RON. Good.

RICHARD. Terrific.

AL. I am also aware that I don't have to sign anything until I'm certain that Wanda's post-natal needs will be met.

RON. Absolutely. Richard?

RICHARD. I'm in total agreement there.

RON. Let's also stay aware that Richard and Rachel can not be held responsible for non-post-natal needs.

AL. It depends on what you consider a non-post-natal need.

RICHARD. Several things.

RON. Let's go back. Let's back up here. Besides medical care, Al, what else do you project that you'll need?

AL. We need a car.

RICHARD. Absolutely not.

AL. How am I supposed to get Wanda to her post-natal care?

RICHARD. Don't dick around with me, Al. You want transportation? I'll kick in for a rental. But no way am I buying you a brand new car. But if you push it, if you push it, my friend, I'm pulling out. I end it now and you can pay the fucking hospital bill.

(A beat.)

AL. Bullshit.

RICHARD. You want to test me? You want to test me? Go right ahead.

AL. I said bullshit. You already put down a bunch of money, you ain't gonna go to someone else and start all over again.

RICHARD. This is sick! This isn't some deal, this is a baby we're talking about! Where the fuck is your humanity?

AL. You want to talk about humanity, Mister? Let's talk about the fact that I'm too poor to keep my baby. Let's talk about the fact that you came to my wife, / you made a deal.

RICHARD. Your wife came to us!

AL. If this ain't a deal then what the fuck are all these contracts about, huh? How come you're bringing your shyster lawyer into this?

RON. Let me just say something here...

AL. *(To Ron.)* Fuck you. You're makin' more money off this than any of us!

RICHARD. *(To Al.)* You're the one, my friend, you're the one who's making on / this deal.

AL. I make nothing! I get nothing / from this!

RICHARD. You're gonna try to get us much as you can from us and then you're gonna call it off. Hey, let's see if we can get a car out of the poor dumb fucks then later we can sell it for her college education!

AL. We don't operate that way, Mister! Maybe that's how you Jews in L.A. think.

RICHARD. Us "Jews"? Us *Jews*? You piece of shit!

AL. I've met people like you! You're a bunch of / shyster schemers.

RICHARD. You have never met people like me, you bastard / piece of shit!

AL. That's why you have all the money! All you want to do is fuck the rest of us over!

RICHARD. I pity you, my friend and I pity your wife and I pity the rest of your backward, ignorant children!

(AL takes a swing at Richard. RICHARD ducks, yells for Ron.)

RON. *(Breaking them up.)* All right, all right! Time out! Hey! Al!

(The PHONE rings. RON reaches for it.)

RON. *(Into phone.)* Yes?... hold on, please. *(HE hands the phone to Richard.)*

RICHARD. Hello?...Ma. How'd you get this number?...uh-huh...no, nothing yet, we're still waiting. Everything's going fine...Yeah, it's a very nice hospital... Ma? I'm in the middle of something...no, we're in the woman's room... Ma, can I call you back?...I will as soon as we know. I promise. I promise, OK, bye-bye.

(RICHARD hangs up. A long beat.)

RICHARD. *(To Al.)* What can I say? You will always have the advantage over me, my friend. You have the ability to make life. *(To Ron.)* Whatever he wants, work it out with him. *(To Al.)* Just so you know, my own car is a Honda. *(RICHARD walks out the door.)*

(RON takes out a yellow pad and looks at Al.)

AL. Forget it. Forget about the car. All I want are some new tires. My tires are shot.
RON. Is that it?

(AL nods.)

RON. We'll figure a hundred a piece, a hundred twenty five to be safe?
AL. That's fine.
RON. And you'll sign to that?
AL. Yeah.
RON. *(Makes a note on a pad.)* I'll have them write this in for you.
AL. They're gonna have something for the baby, aren't they? I mean, some kind of record of us for when she's old enough to know?
RON. Yes.
AL. Would you give them a picture of me? To put in the file?
RON. Sure.

(AL flips through his wallet, looking for pictures. HE pulls out his driver's license, tears the photo off and hands it to Richard.)

RON. Your driver's license...

AL. It's expired. *(Picks up the flowers that fell to the floor during the fight.)* Give these to Wanda when she comes out.

RON. Of course. *(Extending his hand.)* It was nice to meet you, Al.

AL. *(Ignoring his hand.)* Tell Wanda I'll be by later. *(AL walks out.)*

RON. *(Looks out in the hall.)* Richard?

(RICHARD comes back in.)

RON. Well. I think it's set.

RICHARD. *(Still upset.)* Could you give me a second, I just need a second.

RON. Would you like me to leave...?

RICHARD. No, I'll be all right. I'm all right. *(A beat.)* I was thinking out there...my parents, as crazy as their marriage was, you know what they did when they wanted to have a child? My father would take my mother to a supper club. They would have a nice dinner, maybe a little champagne to get my mother silly, then the band would start up and my father, with his enormous belly, he'd take my mother around the dance floor until she fell in love with him all over again. Then he'd bring her home to their bed and together they'd make a baby. He didn't have to drive to a lab on his lunch hour and spill himself into a plastic cup. He didn't have to humble himself in front of a... (*HE waves his hand in Al's direction.*) I just thank God my father is not around to witness this. That's all I can say.

RON. Richard, this is the hardest part. I promise, you won't have any more dealings...

RICHARD. I'm all right. I'll be all right. I'd just appreciate if this was kept between... [us]

RON. (*Immediately.*) Of course.

RICHARD. So. What's the damage?

RON. Four tires. Five hundred bucks.

RICHARD. You're shitting me. How'd you do it?

(*RON throws his hands up and smiles.*)

RICHARD. You don't think he'll change his mind?

RON. No. I don't think so.

RICHARD. Well, good. Thank you.

(*RICHARD goes to shake his hand, then THEY give each other a quick guy-hug.*)

RICHARD. Jesus, I'm exhausted.

RON. It's an exhausting ordeal.

RICHARD. (*Laughing.*) I'm complaining now, wait 'til I'm getting up at four in the morning.

RON. *Oh* yeah. With my son, I didn't get a full night's sleep for two years.

RICHARD. Forget it, the way I worry? With a girl? I won't be sleeping the rest of my life.

RACHEL. (*Enters.*) Richard? Wanda had the baby.

RICHARD. She did? Oh my God. (*RICHARD hugs Rachel.*) We have a baby! (*To Ron.*) I can get excited now?

RON. Absolutely.

RICHARD. (*To Rachel.*) Where is she?

RACHEL. She's in the nursery. The doctor needs to talk to us.

RICHARD. What's wrong?

RACHEL. Everything's OK.

RICHARD. But what?

RACHEL. The cord, the birth cord was shorter than it should have been.

RICHARD. Jesus, they didn't know this before? They didn't know in the amnio?

RACHEL. The baby is fine, she's fine, Richard. (*Very factual.*) When Wanda was pushing down to get her out, the cord was stretched and the oxygen couldn't get through, like a hose that gets bent and the water can't get through. They did a test, the oxygen hadn't been getting through.

RICHARD. But the baby's all right?

RACHEL. She's breathing on her own, now.

RICHARD. They gave her oxygen from the tank and everything?

RACHEL. Yes. And the doctor had me rub her back to help her heart. She cried. She opened one of her hands and shut her fingers around my pinky...

RICHARD. So she'll be all right?

RACHEL. The doctor said there might be some damage.

RICHARD. What kind of damage?

RACHEL. Development damage.

RICHARD. Jesus. So what does this mean, she could be retarded?

RACHEL. She's still a healthy baby, Richard. In every other way, she's perfect.

RICHARD. Rachel, did the doctor say she'd be retarded?

RACHEL. She could be perfectly normal. We don't know.

RICHARD. Did he give a percent?

RACHEL. He doesn't know.

RICHARD. He can't do tests? (*To Ron.*) They can't do a test?

RON. I've had some clients...the tests aren't definitive, no.

RICHARD. So how do we know?

RACHEL. We'll have to wait until she's older.

RICHARD. How much older?

RON. I think at this point we should hear what the doctor has to / say...

RACHEL. Richard, they let me hold her, and as soon as they put her in my arms I felt her body get a little heavier, like suddenly she was relaxed, like she knew she was supposed to be with me. I swear to God, Richard, I felt that.

RICHARD. Where's the doctor?

RACHEL. He's still with Wanda.

RICHARD. (*To Ron.*) Can you stay a little longer?

RON. Of course.

RACHEL. And you know what's strange? She looks a little like you. She looks like that picture we have, of you and Zeda when you were a baby?

RICHARD. Yeah? (*Looking to Ron.*) Maybe we should all take a break, get something to eat...

RON. That's a good idea. There's a cafeteria...

RICHARD. (*To Rachel.*) Honey, you look exhausted. You want to go somewhere and lay down for a minute?

RACHEL. Come see the baby with me.

RON. Rachel, I think this is a good time for all of us to take a breath, give ourselves some time to think...

RACHEL. Richard.

RICHARD. Honey, we need to talk. This child could have some very big problems.

RACHEL. But we don't know that.

RICHARD. Worst case. I'm talking worst case.

RON. I think what Richard is trying to do is to go over all the possibilities...

RACHEL. Richard, I held the baby...

RICHARD. I know.

RACHEL. She was in my arms, I saw her face...

RICHARD. Honey, I know, but what if after a year she can barely sit up in her crib? What if the damage is severe?

RACHEL. Then we'll take it from there.

RICHARD. I don't know if I can do that. I need to know this child is normal.

RACHEL. You can never know a thing like that. My God, that's part of having a baby.

RON. Absolutely. But in our situation we do have other options.

RICHARD. That's what I'm saying. Rachel, if this was our own, of course, but this is not our child.

RACHEL. (*Furious.*) But we can't have our own. We will never have our own. That argument has nothing to do with what is going on / here.

RICHARD. Rachel, what I'm / trying to say...

RACHEL. I don't want to walk away without a baby in my arms. I don't want to do that anymore.

RICHARD. Honey, / I know.

RACHEL. Her room is all ready. I folded the blankets, they're in her crib. I don't want to go home and look at an / empty crib.

RICHARD. Rachel, honey, listen. I'm not saying that it's over. I'm saying that if we've waited this long, we can wait for when it's right. Why should we jump into something and then have our hearts broken even more?

RACHEL. We can't just walk out. We made a promise to these / people...

RICHARD. Honey, we'll do what we have to do. (*To Ron.*) What are our obligations?

RON. If nothing is signed...

RICHARD. Then we don't have to take her?

RON. No.

RICHARD. Is this done?

RON. All the time.

RACHEL. Jesus, Richard, we can't just abandon her. This is still a life.

RON. I don't think it would be considered abandonment. First of all, the child has its natural parents...

RACHEL. What if they don't take her?

RICHARD. That's not our responsibility.

RACHEL. I can't believe you're saying this.

RICHARD. They could have taken the baby away from us at any time. *Any time.* You think that baby was ever really ours?

RACHEL. I'm asking about the baby. What happens to her if they don't want her?

RON. She'll be put up for adoption.

RICHARD. Someone else will take her.

RACHEL. Who? Who's going to take a child like this?

RON. Oh geez, you'd be surprised. All kinds of couples like to take in kids with special needs. There's a couple I read about with a ranch, they devote their lives...*Sixty Minutes* did a thing...

RICHARD. That's right, I saw it. (*To Rachel.*) We saw it...

RACHEL. For God's sake Richard!

RICHARD. Rachel, if we wanted a retarded baby, we could have gotten one at no expense. And I'm not talking about the money, sweetheart, I'm talking about the heartache, and the worrying, and all the crap that these two people have put us through. I put up with it because there was going to be joy at the end of all of it. There will be no joy with a child / like this...

RACHEL. We don't know that.

RICHARD. But what if? What if?

RACHEL. She still have a soul, Richard, this is a child we can love.

(RICHARD takes RACHEL in his arms. SHE's holding on to him. THEY're both moving around each other, almost is if they were in a dance step.)

RICHARD. Rachel, please, when we've talked about our child, what did we talk / about?

RACHEL. I know.

RICHARD. We didn't talk about having a genius, we talked about having a regular kid...

RACHEL. Richard, I know.

RICHARD. ...who would take walks with us / and ask millions of questions, and the magic of taking her to her first play and what if God forbid she wants to be an actress...

RACHEL. We *have* a child, that other child does not exist, I want *this* child.

RICHARD. Honey, she's not the only one...

RACHEL. They gave her to me to hold...

RICHARD. I know...

RACHEL. ...she held my finger, / she opened her eyes to me, she looked at my face, I could smell her skin, she cried to me...

RICHARD. I want a child I can teach the alphabet to and take on hikes. I didn't go through all of this for a kid who might sit in a corner and rock her knees / all day.

RACHEL. I FELT HER BREATH.

(A beat.)

. RICHARD. *(Barely audible.)* I can't do it , Rachel.
RACHEL. Won't you even look at her?

(RICHARD shakes her head.)

RACHEL. I can't raise this child alone, Richard. I can't
have her be a stranger to you. I won't allow that.

(RICHARD doesn't say anything.)

RACHEL. Then are you willing to do this again? Are
you willing to go out and find someone else and do this
whole thing over again? Because I need to have a baby.
RICHARD. If that's what you want.
RON. I have a girl in Virginia. She's due in less than
two weeks. She's single, eighteen, a receptionist, very
bright. Boyfriend, who's the father, is a college grad.
(Rooting in his briefcase.) In fact I think I have a picture of
her...The couple I had for her just pulled out.

(RON hands RICHARD the picture.)

RON. She had an amnio. Very healthy. Vegetarian.
RACHEL. Could Richard and I be alone for a minute,
Ron?
RON. Absolutely. If you need me, I'll be out in the
hall.
RICHARD. Thank you.

(RON exits. A beat.)

RICHARD. Do you want me to go look at the baby?
RACHEL. No.

(A beat.)

    RICHARD. What do you want to do?
    RACHEL. I don't know.
    RICHARD. *(The picture of the girl.)* Do you want to
look at this?

*(RACHEL shakes her head. RICHARD lets the picture go
    and it falls to the ground.)*

FADE OUT

Scene 2

*A while later. LIGHTS UP on WANDA in bed. RACHEL
is sitting next to her in a chair. Neither one of them are
saying anything. A large, expensive floral arrangement
is on the bedside table.*

    WANDA. You can take your flowers back if you want.
    RACHEL. Wanda, I wouldn't do that. *(A beat.)* Do you
want me to take them out?
    WANDA. They take flowers at the chapel.
    RACHEL. All right. I'll take care of that before I go.
(A beat.) Do you know what you're going to do?
    WANDA. What time does your airplane leave?
    RACHEL. Wanda, I'd like to help you keep the baby.
    WANDA. Money ain't gonna fix it.
    RACHEL. Please, let me help you keep your child.
    WANDA. And how are you gonna do that? You gonna
buy her a bunch of clothes? You gonna send her to a
special school? You gonna find her a room to sleep in?

OK, you do that. What about my other kids? What's supposed to happen to the rest of my kids? You can't fix this, Rachel. There ain't nothing you can fix here. Just go home. Just go on home.

(AL has entered. HE stands by the door, waiting for Rachel to leave.)

RACHEL. *(Barely audible.)* I'm sorry. *(Exits.)*

WANDA. Where'd you take the kid?

AL. The Pizza Hut.

WANDA. That's good. They like it there.

AL. I gave them some quarters so they could play with the video games.

WANDA. That's good, honey. I talked to Mama.

AL. What'd you tell her?

WANDA. I told her the baby didn't make it.

AL. What'd she say?

WANDA. She said that I shouldn't feel sad because the baby was now with the Lord Jesus. Did you look at her Al? Is she pretty?

AL. Yeah, she's a pretty baby.

WANDA. People like pretty babies. Was she crying?

AL. No.

WANDA. What if I asked to see the baby. I could hold her in my arms and sing to her 'til she falls asleep. Then I'd lay a pillow over her head and let her soul go up to God. Someone will take her, won't they, Al?

AL. Sure they will, Babe.

WANDA. Look how flat my belly is. I never noticed that before. You know how I always have my babies laying on top of me? You know how I like to take naps with a baby on my belly. Feel by belly, Al, there's nothing there.

(WANDA starts to wail. AL crawls into the bed with Wanda and covers her body with his.)

FADE OUT

END OF PLAY

COSTUME PLOT

WANDA:
Pregnancy padding,
Maternity dress and slip
Purse

RACHEL:
Scarf
Purse
Sunglasses & case
Jacket (Act II)

RICHARD:
Jacket
Shirt
Tie
Eyeglasses & case

AL:
Cap
Sunglasses

RON:
Jacket
2 shirts
Tie
Dialing watch

PROPERTY PLOT

ONSTAGE:
Sofa bed (open, cushions on floor SR of sofa)
   on: 2 pillows
          sheets
          Wanda's sweat jacket (SR arm)
Cardboard wardrobe (door open to TV tray)
Armchair
   on: lamp
          1 picture (large pink frame)
Coffee table
   on: ashtray
TV stool
   on: TV
          on: 2 pictures (smaller frames)
Dining table
   on: 4 place settings; SL w/placemats
          fork (for cold cut plate)
          folded paper towel on plates
          telephone (DR corner)
          ashtray (center of table)
          kitchen matches (center of table)
          pack of cigarettes (center of table)
3 chairs at table
Short stool under table (DS side)
Refrigerator
   in: water jar
          3 Jello cups (1 parfait, 2 cups)
          Cool Whip container
          cold cut plate
          mayonnaise jar (in door)
          mustard container (in door)
          ice cubes in bowl (in freezer)
   on front: picture (no frame, Brian)

                    crayon drawings
Step stool
    on: Wanda's purse
          in: car keys
                  newspaper ad
Baby high chair (behind refrigerator)

Counter Unit:

    on stove:
          frying skillet
          empty pan
          pan w/coffee on UL burner)
    in drying rack (SL of sink):
          2 coffee cups
          4 glasses
          spoon
    top shelf under stove:
          Saran wrap
          extra silverware
    under sink:
          flower can
    shelf above sink:
          can of peaches
    SR of sink:
          loaf of bread
    US of sink:
          2 sponges
    US of stove:
          box of toothpicks
          salt & pepper shakers
    DS of stove:
          sugar bowl w/spoon
          garbage can (by DS end of counter)
          dump bucket (in bathroom)

OFFSTAGE:

Fan
Bible for Wanda
1 cigarette (Wanda)
Flower arrangement
Plastic glass w/water & bendable straw

PROP TABLE:

Beer can (open; 1/3 full)
Cigarettes (for Wanda)
Lighter (for cigarettes)
Rachel's Williams Sonoma bag
   in: cassette tape in case
          photo album
          pre-natal vitamins
          wrapped gift box
          in: maternity dress
                   slip
                   tissue paper (taped to box)
          flowers (in paper & tied)
Rachel's purse
   in: compact
          pocket book (w/checks & pen)
          photos (in envelope)
          sunglasses (in case)
Al's grocery bag
   in: 6 pack of 3 Cokes & 3 7-UP
          1 daisy
          6 pack of beer for Al
Baby bag
   in: water bottle
          camera

stuffed animal
1 baby bottle
Rachel's purse (for Act II)
Car seat w/baby blanket
3 carnations (tied w/string for Al)
3 cups coffee

PERSONAL PROPS:

RICHARD:
Airline tickets (right outer jacket pocket)
Beeper
Cash (in pant's pocket)
Briefcase
    in: *Variety*
          New York Times
          Tic-tacs
          micro cassette recorder
          tooth brush
          tooth paste
          razor
          glasses in case
          fountain pen
          checkbook
          Maalox bottle (2/3 full)

RON:
Wallet
    in: business cards
"dialing" watch
coins
Briefcase (brown)
    in: clean, unwrapped shirt
          computer
          legal pad

              picture of girl
              Cross pen
              3 sets of contracts (in manilla folder)
              (consisting of Custody agreement; Interstate
              agreement, California agreement)
Extra business cards

AL:
Wallet
    in: drivers license
Sunglasses

Between I:1 and I:2

SHIFT:
—close sofa bed and replace cushions
—move 2 pillows to armchair
—move coffee table US
—move ashtray from table to US of dry rack
—move matches, cigarettes, & lighter to DS of dry rack

SET:
—fan on TV tray (DS of lamp)
—"Cool Whip" tub of ice (in front of fan)

STRIKE:
—crushed can (by Al)
—newspaper ad (by Al)
—tabloids/newspapers from dining table

INTERMISSION

II:1
ONSTAGE:
hospital bed (made; head cranked even w/headboard)

on: 1 pillow
bedside table (SL of bed)
    on: telephone
          tissue box
trash can (SL of bedside table)
rolling table (SR of bed)
    on: water pitcher (2/3 full)
          2 glasses
table (SR)
2 chairs (US & DS of table; DS chair facing SL)
baby bassinet (SL)
armchair (DSL)

Bathroom:
sink
towel on rack
toilet
wastebasket

Between II:1 and II:2

SHIFT:
—move US chair (at table) to SL of bed
—straighten mattress

SET:
glass w/water & straw (on rolling table)
flower arrangement (on bedside table)

STRIKE:

briefcase
baby bag
surgical gown
picture (if possible)

shirt wrapping
Ron's shirt (from bathroom door)

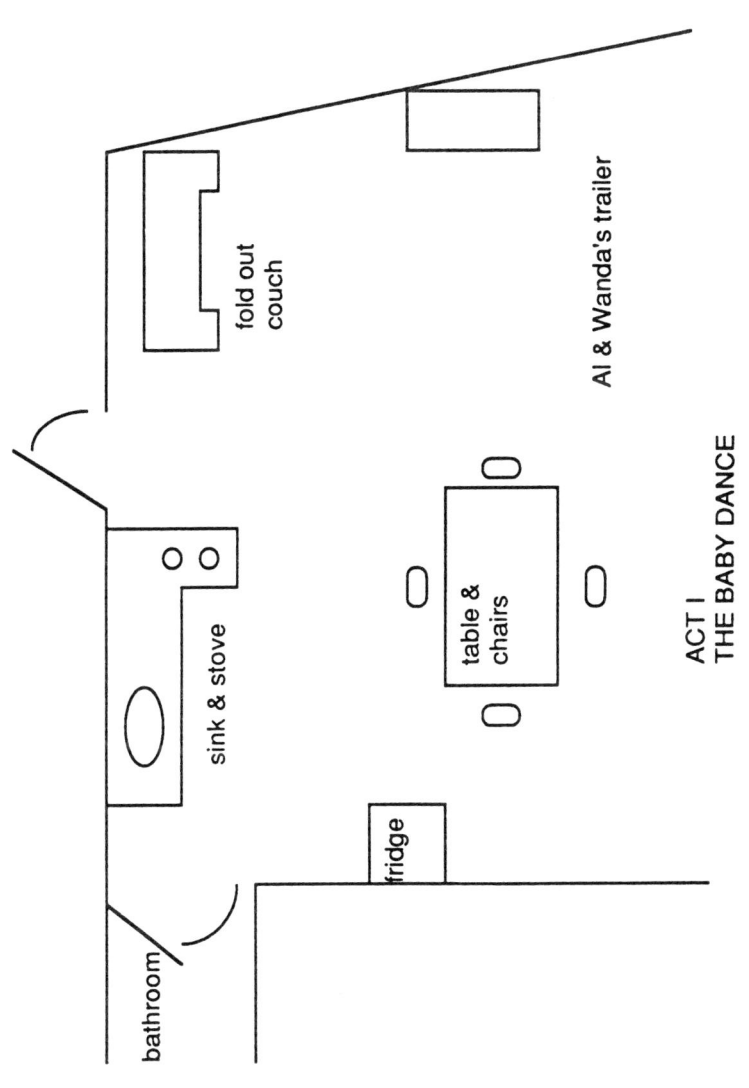

fold out
couch

sink & stove

bathroom

fridge

table &
chairs

Al & Wanda's trailer

ACT I
THE BABY DANCE

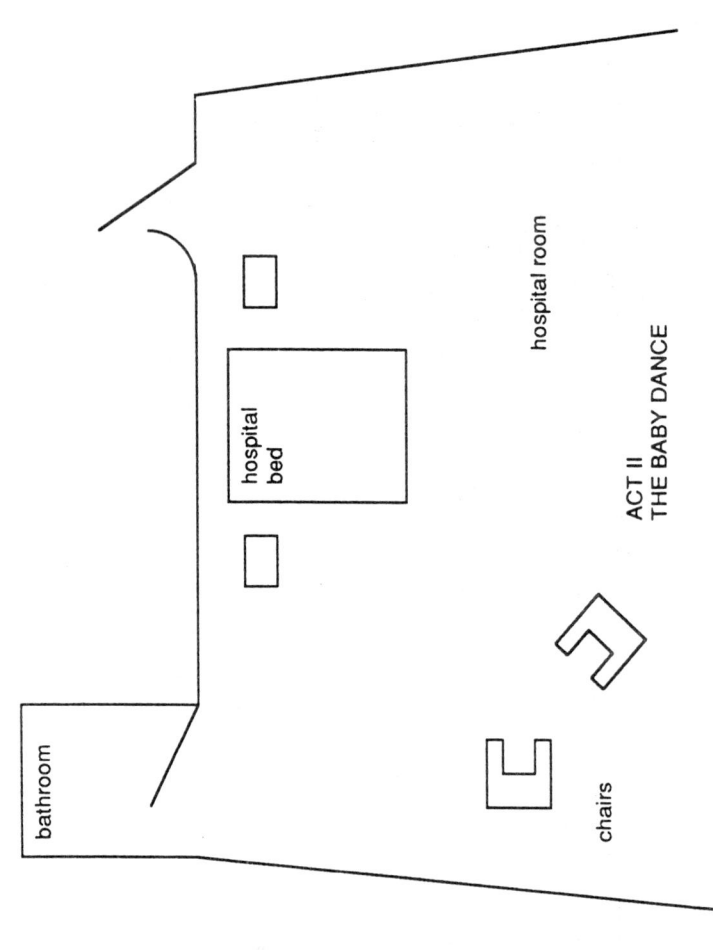

bathroom

hospital bed

hospital room

chairs

ACT II
THE BABY DANCE

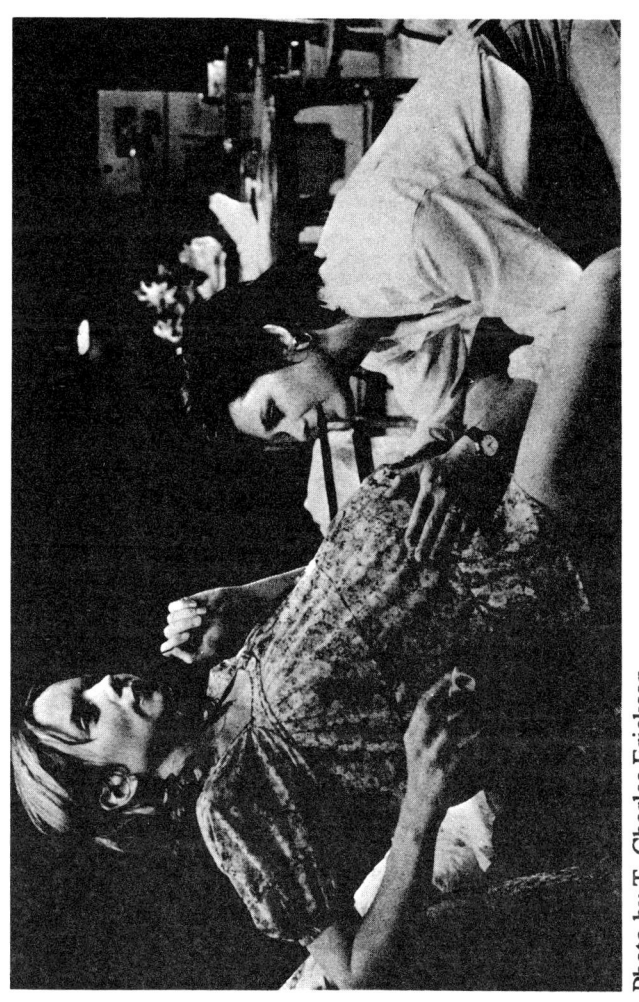

Photo by T. Charles Erickson

Other Publications for Your Interest

THE VOICE OF THE PRAIRIE
(LITTLE THEATRE—COMIC/DRAMA)
By JOHN OLIVE

2 men, 1 women—to play a variety of roles
May be done with up to 10 actors—Unit Setting

When this play begins, we are listening to an old hobo (named "Poppy" by his avid companion young Davey Quinn) tell a tall tale. It is the early 1890's, and itinerant story tellers such as Poppy really were the voices of the prairie. Many years later, when Davey is grown up, he is "discovered" by radio entrepreneur Leon Schwab, telling his tales of Poppy and of Frankie the Blind Girl, whom he rescued from a cruel father and with whom he went on a cross-country adventure. Schwab thinks Quinn's stories would attract an audience for radio, the "wave of the future". Sure enough, David Quinn becomes famous as the Voice of the Prairie, as the cleverly-constructed play cross-cuts between scenes of Leon and David and scenes of young Davey and Frankie the Blind Girl, on the lam, in search of adventure. These scenes culminate in the unfortunate separation of Davey and Frankie, as Frankie is recognized, captured and sent back home. David Quinn, the grown-up Voice of the Prairie, has not seen or heard from her since; until, that is, Leon locates her in hopes of using his discovery of the actual, famous Frankie the Blind Girl for its sentimental value, to keep the new F.C.C. off his back. Will David forgive Frankie for leaving him so many years ago? Will Frankie agree to help Leon avoid jail for broadcasting without a license? "Endearing."—N.Y. Times. "That rare thing: a small, skillful play with a deft heart."—Los Angeles Times. "Beguiling entertainment and as American as corn."—Hartford Advocate. "First-rate entertainment. I can't remember when I last so enjoyed a play."—Torrington Register Citizen. Slightly Restricted.

(#24047)

CARELESS LOVE
(LITTLE THEATRE—DRAMA)
By JOHN OLIVE

1 male, 1 woman—Unit set

What a terrific little play for an actress and actor to sink their teeth into! And, it's about something that matters: commitment, and responsibility, in love. When we first meet Jack, he is an aspiring actor, serious about his career but not very serious about his girlfriend, Martha, a waitress who is an aspiring dancer, who is a lot more serious about Jack. The couple drifts along on a cloud of good times — until Martha gets pregnant, at which time a *Choice* must be made. As the debate over their options progresses, Jack's acting career starts to take off; and, he starts to think more seriously about his life and his responsibilities. Unfortunately, at the same time Martha has been driven into self-absorption by Jack's carelessness, and has made a decision which is right for her, she thinks: she has decided to give the child up for adoption. So — at just about the time Jack is ready to make an emotional committment to Martha and to their child, it is too late: Martha has had the baby and put it up for adoption. This was, after all, *her* decision to make. Right? In the end, Martha is a self-sufficient contemporary woman, who makes her own choices. It is Jack who will hurt forever, from the pain of eternal separation from his child. "Bittersweet." — Variety. "In the delicacy of its writing, in the truth of its details...it is a most lovely, most satisfying evening in the theatre."—Chicago Tribune. "A lovely little play...works a winsome magic."—Philadelphia Daily News.

(#5237)